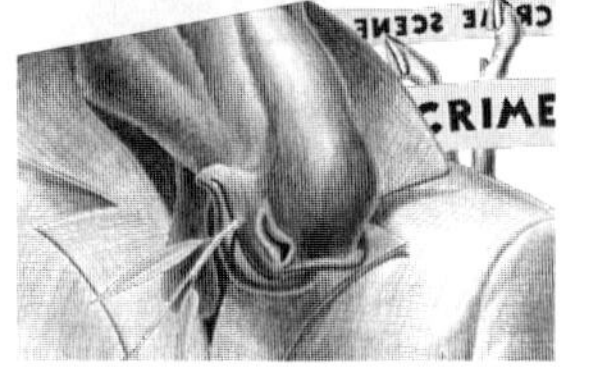

Moose

A Detective Story

Praise for other books by Tom Lang

coffee

"**...**an engaging story and it has literary merit. The book is a little like espresso. It's small, tightly packed and full of flavor...as good as anything you find out of New York."
— Doug Dutton, Dutton's Books, Los Angeles

cat

"Tom Lang's **cat** offers a deceptively deep and complex story in the guise of a simple tale about a reformed cat hater and his feline, Bouhaki. Lang paints his characters with deft strokes, sweetly hooking his unsuspecting reader's heart."
— Shannon Brownlee, senior editor, U.S. News & World Report

eagle

"Absolutely hilarious! By combining comedy with facts, Lang has created a unique and clever look at eagles and their private lives."
— Alaska Raptor Rehabilitation Center, Sitka, Alaska

mrs. claus

"...destined to become a holiday classic...a painfully funny story about the true meaning of giving and family
— Joe Kurmaskie, *Metal Cowboy*

For Molly Jean

May you create your own destiny

Also by Tom lang

Coffee
Cat
Eagle
Salmon
Bear
Mrs. Claus

Published by Boudelang Press:
www.boudelang.com
www.tomlangbooks.com

Email tomlangbooks@gmail.com

TEL 310-712-5606

PO Box 852 Haines, AK 99827

Design by Nancy Phillips Design
Editor Laurie Insley

ISBN # 978-0-9649742-5-8

SHE WALKED INTO MY OFFICE, all 800 pounds of sweet lean Alaskan moose sashaying my way. A light rust tint sparkled off her golden brown hair. She bent over, stripped a willow branch with her mouth and ate slow, like I wasn't there. She looked up at me. Water lilies danced in the swampy ponds of her eyes.

"I'm Cervida and I'm missing my male."

"I'll bet he's missing you, too."

"That's not what I mean. He's missing. Gone."

"How long has he been gone?"

"Three days."

"That's not long."

"It is for one of my bulls. I tell my males when it's time to be missing and when it's time to be gone."

She turned sideways to grab an alder leaf so I grabbed a look at her body. Her humped shoulder, pale long legs and big head with her overhanging snout sent shivers through the dewlap under my chin. She stepped next to me and looked me up and down.

"You're tall."

I'm a hoof over seven feet at the shoulders and I'm a good 10 feet long.

"Bigger than average," I said.

She nudged my antlers.

"Nice rack. How big is it?"

I flared out my chest and extended my neck so she could get a good look at my six foot wide antlers.

"Way bigger than average," I said.

"I've heard that before," Cervida said, turning to eat more leaves.

"Look, you beautiful cow, you're not here to give me a physical and this ain't no restaurant. So, what can I do for you?"

"I hear you're the best."

"Best at what?"

"Finding things."

"I'm not bad."

"No, you're not."

She chewed the leaf slowly as we stood staring at each other.

"Are you free to find my male?"

"I ain't free and I ain't cheap."

"Neither am I," she said.

I stripped a branch from above me and chewed and stared while she chewed and stared back.

"Sure, Ms. Cervida—"

"Call me Vida."

"Okay, Vida, I'll graze around and see what I can find."

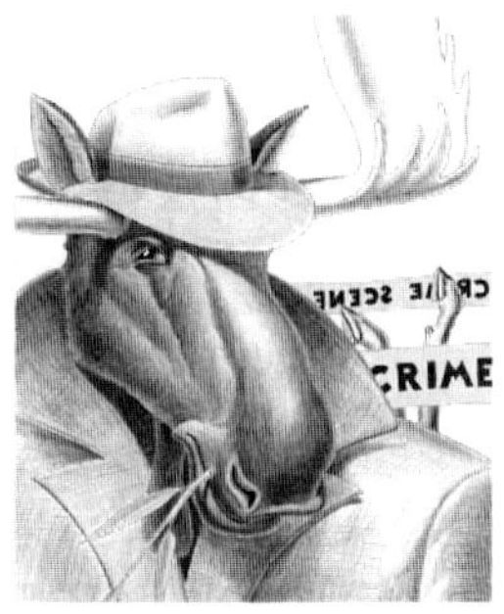

I'M AL GIGAS, MOOSE DETECTIVE. I've roamed the mean riverbeds of the Chilkat Valley for ten years and I've seen things no creature should ever see and I've seen creatures that will never see again.

A missing moose is a bad sign but I didn't mention that to Vida. She wasn't the first ungulate to walk into my office looking for a loved one. I've had brothers looking for brothers, calves for mothers, mothers for calves. I find things, Vida was right about that. But what I find this time of year would be better if it stayed lost.

October was almost here. The wind starts blowing out of the north, the kind of wind that raises the inch-long hair on your rump and sends a sick feeling down into your large rumen, the biggest of my four stomachs. When the fall wind blows any meadow can explode with a moose battle; a misunderstood bellow can end with a fight to the death. The north wind tells a moose that winter is coming and life is about to get tougher. And if you're a moose in the Chilkat Valley you know that the wind is telling you the killings are about to begin.

"MUWAH! MUWAH!"

I was thinking less about Vida's male and more about the way she swayed out of my office when I heard the moose call from up valley. Thinking this might have something to do with my case, I trotted up the flats of the Chilkat River, my stomachs growling for food. Vida paid me my usual retainer of 300 pounds of wet forage and I could sure use it. I go through 40 to 50 pounds a day during the summer but as fall nears I can put away 100 pounds a day.

A herd of moose ahead of me milled around in the shallows of the river near a stand of alders. Two bulls together usually means trouble. More than two bulls together means big trouble. Sheriff Winkle stood in front of the others, staring down at the brown, silty river water.

"How are you doing, Sheriff?"

"How am I doing, Gigas? How am I doing? I got more internal parasites than a porcupine's got quills. I got flukes, nematodes and bot flies. I'm a walking worm factory. I got tapeworms, whipworms, bladder worms, nodular worms and lungworms. My lower front teeth are as dull as my brain but not sharp like my upper front teeth."

"Moose don't have upper front teeth, Sheriff."

"You're sharp, Gigas. You should be a detective."

The sheriff pointed his antlers toward the moose crowd.

"Go tell us what you think about the mess over there, detective."

I knew what I thought and I knew what I was going to find and I knew it wasn't going to be pretty. No matter how many times you see it you never get used to seeing a member of your species massacred. I walked to the moose, the herd stepping back to let me through.

"Lots of blood," I said

"Blood! I knew it!" someone said.

I looked up. There's always one dumb moose in the crowd.

"That could have been me," a moose said, his voice shaking.

"Could have been any one of us," I said, "and next time it will be one of us."

The moose mooed a collective moo.

"What kind of animal would do something like this?"

I shrugged my shoulders as I circled the drying pool of blood. I could tell the victim was a bull because of the tracks. A male moose has a longer hoof because he tends to be a third larger than a female. A male hoof is also blunter at the front end whereas a female hoof has a sharp point. A cow track has a circular outline but a bull track is more oblong. I knew he had tried to run away from his killer because of the wide stride marks in the mud. Our walking stride is 3.5 to 5.5 feet but when we trot or run our stride lengthens to 8 feet.

"Hmm," I said.

"What's that mean?" a voice behind me asked.

"It means 'hmm.' It also means our victim was surprised and he tried to run away before he was attacked."

"How do you know?"

"Lucky guess."

I followed the death stain, the mixture of blood and mud forming a cloudy sunset on the ground. The trail ended in a set of familiar tracks. Tire tracks, from a human truck. A flash of lightning stung my brain and I stumbled, memory kicking up swirls of dust in my head.

"You okay, Al?"

I steadied myself and nodded my antlers.

"Yeah, just lost my footing is all. Just lost my footing."

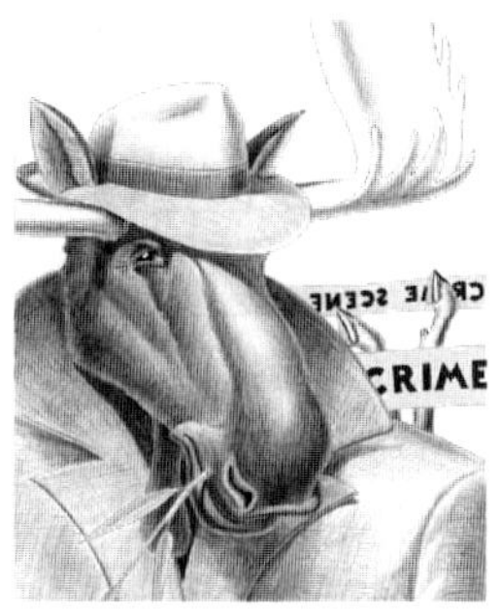

COWS ARE MY WEAKNESS, and of all the valleys in all of Alaska and the Yukon, she had to walk into mine. Male moose are able to mate at two-years-old but I was almost four and I hadn't mated yet even though I told my friends that I had. Not that I hadn't tried, but the older bulls were too tough. They intimidated me, pushed me around, kicked mud in my face.

I was walking through the brush during

mating season, late September, resigning myself to a loveless life when I stopped in my tracks. I lifted my chin, stretched my neck, opened my mouth wide. The nasal organ in my upper palate pumped mucus and I captured a whiff of airborne chemicals telling me a female was nearby. The old Flehman's Response.

She stepped out of the trees into the clearing in the meadow. She was thin and frail. Her two inch tail wagged back and forth, her long ears turned in the wind. I got a case of the gulps and she turned toward me.

"Oh, great, another one," she said.

She turned up her overhanging nose and lip.

"How unusual. A salivating, chomping, lip-smacking male moose that makes a hollow gulping sound every two seconds. How charming. I feel faint."

Embarrassed, I wiped my mouth on the brush.

"Let me guess. You're going to create a shallow depression in the ground, paw the earth into a muddy mess and expect me to lie down and roll around in it?"

"Hey, I'm only out for a walk and you walked into my path."

"Then keep walking and don't get any ideas."

I walked a few steps away from her and stopped, full of ideas.

"Uh, do you like pond scum?"

"Is this a trick question? Who doesn't?"

Nervous, I looked down and kicked a few rocks.

"I know a spot that has the best pond scum in the valley and I thought you might…want to come along."

She gave me the moose stare. I looked up at the sky, down valley, up valley. I stole a sideways glance at her. She was still staring.

"Well?"

"Don't rush me, I'm thinking. Well, okay, that sounds good. I've been eating willow all day and I'm sick of it. But, hey, keep your hooves to yourself."

We walked in silence through the woods, stopping now and then to nibble on the fading flora. When we came to the watering hole she jumped in.

"Oh, yum, delicious," she said, her snout stained green. "It's so salty. I love it."

The way she slurped at the algae made me wish I was pond scum.

"The food in the ponds and lakes has 400 times the salt of the twigs we eat during the winter,"

I told her. "That's why we need to stock up on sodium rich foods during the summer and fall."

"You're a smart one," she said.

"I know things."

"Hmm."

"What's that mean?"

"It means, 'hmm'," she said.

We spent the next few days grazing from pond to pond and slough to slough. She was nervous and sensitive, jumping at the slightest noises in the night. She told me about her traumatic youth. Most moose are born in late May or early June, but she arrived in July and only weighed 15 pounds, less than half my birth weight. She wasn't even 100 pounds by the fall and she barely survived her first winter. She couldn't remember long segments of her early life until she went to regressive memory therapy and relived seeing a brown bear eat her mother.

She was two and a half years old but she was not much bigger than a yearling and I had an overwhelming drive to protect her. She was stunning and I kept my gulping to a minimum while I was with her but it wasn't easy. I bit my lip to stop chomping and smacking but that's hard to do when you don't have upper front teeth.

I was on my best behavior, waiting for her to give me a sign. One evening we stood near a road, munching on greens, the sky scorched red by the setting sun. She rubbed her rump against mine and whispered in my ear, "Moo-moo-ah, moo-moo-ah."

Are there sweeter words in any language? I romanced her for a week. We rolled in the mud and swam in the rivers. I was singing a song I'd written for her, "My Baby's Got Me in a Rut," when the wind started blowing slowly from the north. She nuzzled up close to me.

"The north wind," she shivered, "it gives me a bad feeling."

"It's just the wind."

We were standing in silence watching the last rays of the sun dip behind the mountains when I heard the clumsy sound of human footsteps. She was still naïve about the dangers of the world and looked upon humans as harmless, funny looking creatures.

I knew better.

"Look," she said, laughing, "they're so…goofy."

Then I saw the flash of metal from the guns.

"Run!" I said. "Follow me!"

I ran through the thicket, breaking small trees in my path. A gunshot blasted through the air, the sound stinging my ears. As the ringing echoed away all I could hear was the lonely sound of my hooves on the soft earth of the rainforest. My stomachs spasmed as I turned my head to look for her. She was laying on the ground, eyes open, blood drooling out her mouth. The approach of human footsteps stole my time to grieve and I ran into the woods until I was exhausted.

I spent the night in the forest, walking in circles, smashing my antlers against tree trunks, hoping that the impact would awaken me from a bad dream. But this was no dream and in the morning my nightmare continued. I walked back to the spot where she had been shot, but her body was gone. I followed her blood trail, sucking in the last wisps of her scent as her sweet smell disappeared into the greenery around me. Then I looked down.

At the tire tracks in the road.

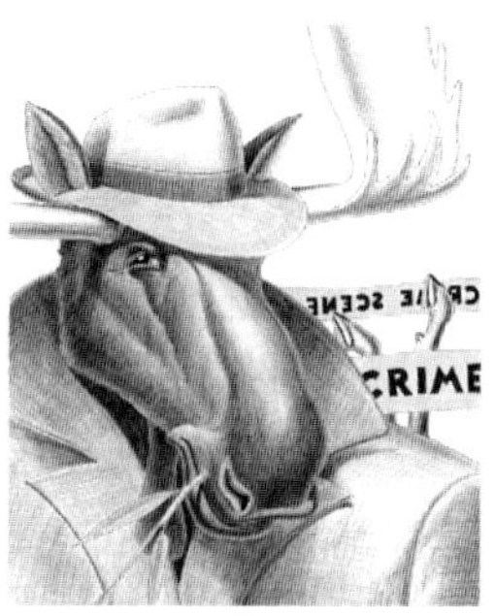

"YOU OKAY, GIGAS?"

The sheriff's voice brought me back from my thoughts.

"Sure, I'm fine."

"Everyone go on about your business," the sheriff told the herd. "It's mating season. Go have some fun, but be careful out there."

The moose bellowed, smacked antlers and headed their own ways. I turned to the sheriff.

"Go have some fun?"

"That's right, Gigas. Let them go have some fun. While they can. You stopped having fun a long time ago."

"What about the murder?"

"What about it? What do you expect me to do? Catch the murderer? Bring him to justice? What world do you live in?"

I shrugged my shoulders.

"Listen, Gigas, you're hired to find missing moose, right, Gigas? Lucky you. I'm hired to keep moose from being missed. Unlucky me. We're just moose and the odds are against us. The sun starts to set on us the day we're born and we have to catch as much daylight as we can before nightfall. I'm here to give some kind of order to the exit line."

"You saying we have no control over our destiny, Sheriff?"

"None, my friend, not a bit. Don't take it personal. It is what it is."

I nodded my head and slowly headed down the river bank.

"Where you going, Al?"

"To take control of my destiny, Sheriff."

"SEE ANYTHING TODAY?"

"Nope, not me. I haven't seen a thing in months."

"I find that hard to believe."

"Believe what you will."

I was talking to Hal, a bald eagle perched on a cottonwood tree with a clear view of the murder scene.

"How's your hearing?" I asked.

"What's that?" Hal said. We looked at each other and chuckled.

"Listen, wise one, a brother moose was killed down by the flats within the last 12 hours. What do you know?"

"I know better than to get involved with the humans during the killing season."

"So the murderer was a human?"

"I didn't say that."

"What are you afraid of? You're an American bald eagle. You're protected."

"Oh, yeah? My cousin mouthed off one too many times and next thing you know his wings are clipped and he's doing life in one of those prisons where the humans stare at you all day."

"Better than having them shoot and stuff you like the old days."

"Just a slower death, Mr. Detective."

The sound of a distant gun shot echoed off the mountains. Hal shook his feathers.

"Too close for me. I'm out of here."

With a flap of his wings Hal dropped off his branch and soared up valley. I snuck through the trees toward the sound of the gun. When I heard the fading murmur of human voices in the woods I stopped and waited for silence. Then I walked into a clearing and stepped into a pool of blood. I shook my legs and tried to wipe them on the ground but the blood had already stained my hooves. An engine started up on the other side of the willows and I ran toward the sound. A white truck was driving away on the dirt road. I wanted to tail the truck and discover where it was going but the dust from the road choked and disoriented me. I lost my footing and slid coughing into a ravine. I looked up into the fog of dirt, blinded by my eternal nightmare.

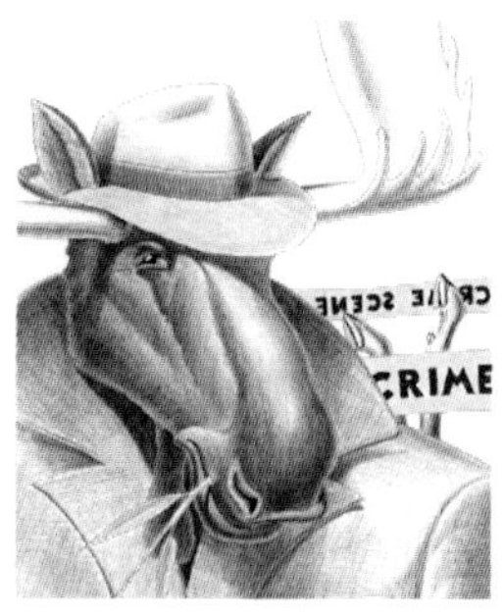

COULD I HAVE DONE ANYTHING to protect her? That's always the question that rips at my heart like a bear claw. Should I have told her to run ahead of me? Should I have charged the humans and caught them off guard? I'm a tough moose, at least that's my reputation. I sent a brown bear to the promise land with a powerful kick to the head. I gored a male alpha wolf with my antlers and tossed him in the river. He wasn't an alpha wolf after that.

What ifs and could have beens banged antlers in my head. The sheriff was right. We're moose. We live 15 years on this earth, we're lucky. We die of old age we're blessed. If the bears don't eat us when we're young they'll eat us when we're old. If the humans don't shoot us when we're at the peak of our lives the wolves will take us down when we're tired and feeble. We're herbivores in a carnivore world. It is what it is.

I walked along the river toward town as twilight dimmed the valley. As I neared town I stood alongside the road tucked back into the trees, scanning the trucks as they came and went. Which truck held the human that killed my love? Which truck was responsible for today's murder? Were all the humans in all the trucks responsible for all the moose murders over the years?

As night settled in around me I crept into town, avoiding the well-lit areas. A light rain patted my coat. I walked the trails between the human homes, looking at trucks and examining the tracks left by their tire treads. Was it this one? No, that one? Maybe that one? The problem was the trucks all looked alike, just like humans all look alike. And if I did find the killer what was I going to do? I'm a moose detective. Just thinking of the species jurisdictional issues gave me a headache.

I stood in a field of dying fireweed and cow's parsnip. The stars shimmered above me and the moon lit up the water in front of me. I looked over the fields of food and tried to understand carnivore mentality. What more could they want than this? I shook my head.

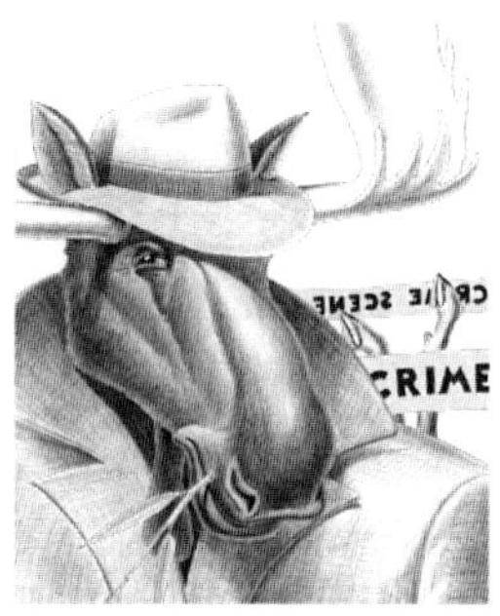

I PACED BACK AND FORTH IN MY office in Moose Meadows for the next few days. I didn't go out. No one came in. I couldn't get the bloodstains off my hooves. My head ached, each gunshot in the distance a dull roar in my head, reminding me of the killings.

The past sat on my chest like a 1200 pound brown bear. I couldn't predict the future and I obviously couldn't forget the past, but I knew I could find Cervida's male if he was still alive. She had given me his general range, a ten mile area between my office and the town. However, to get that close to town during the killing season was suicide this time of year. I might as well hang a "shoot me" sign from my antlers. But I had a job to do.

I knew I would have to stop for lunch nine or ten times, so I walked out of the meadows mid-afternoon and grazed my way toward town. At one point I was spooked by what I thought was a human truck but it was only a car with gray maned humans staring at me. I stared back until they drove off.

Focus, Gigas, I mumbled to myself. I had to be more careful so I moved further into the woods. I looked for moose landmarks: fresh moose scat, newly broken alder branches, muddy, hooved tracks. I stopped for another bite to eat. I knew better than to waste my time chasing a moose. If he was alive he would come my way. I was in his range. I finished chewing and closed my eyes and slowly dozed off.

"I'VE GOT THE HERBIVORE BLUES."
"Moo-moo-ah, moo-moo-ah."
"Tell those carnivores the news."
"Moo-moo-ah, moo-moo-ah."

I was standing at the bar at Rumen's Café. The banner above the stage read: VIDA AND THE DREAM COWS. Cervida sashayed her rump back and forth across the stage as her cows mooed behind her.

"They say it is what it is
That it just beez that way
And if there's no tomorrow
I need some lovin' today
I've got the herbivore blues
Hey, girls, can I get some help?"

The Dream Cows swung their short tails back and forth, singing:

"Moo-moo-ah, moo-moo-ah."

A spotlight followed Vida as she slowly walked off the stage and came my way. The Dream Cows kept the rhythm:

"Moo-moo-ah, moo-moo-ah."
"Tell the carnivores the news
I've got the herbivore blues
Why don't they get a clue
They're giving me, oh,

The carnivores are giving me
The herbivore blues!"

Vida had snuggled in next to me, eye to eye, snout to snout, as she held that last b-flat note. With her this close her female hormones should have filled my nasal cavity with mucus, but there was no Flehman's Response.

Somewhere a twig snapped and woke me from my dream. I spun around. A young, small bull was standing there, squinting at me.

"YOU AL GIGAS?"

"Depends."

"On what?"

"On who you are."

"I'm a friend of Vida and I hear you're looking for me."

"Then I'm Al Gigas."

He bent down and chewed on a few dogwood leaves. There was something soft about him, almost feminine. He was passive, unlike most bulls during the rut, or mating season. If you're a male moose, you not only have to be afraid of the humans, but also of the bulls who battle to win the females.

I looked at him. He circled around me four or five times. His hips were stiff and he bumped into a tree as if he didn't see it. He paused and locked eyes with me and stared.

"Where have you been?" I asked.

"Wandering."

"Wandering where?"

"Nowhere in particular."

He started to circle me again.

"Cervida's worried about you. Thinks you might be hurt."

"I'm okay," he said.

"Right," I said. "As okay as a moose with

parelaphostrongylus tenuis can be."

His neck twitched.

"I don't know what you're talking about," he said as he circled me again.

"Don't play dumb moose with me," I said. "You've got brainworm, a meningeal flatworm common but not fatal in white-tailed deer. In moose, elk and caribou, we're not so lucky. The parasites live in the eyes and in the central nervous system. The symptoms are repetitive circling, aimless wandering, partial paralysis of the hindquarters and partial blindness."

"You're talking out the side of your snout," he said, talking to a low lying limb of a big spruce tree.

"I'm over here," I said.

He turned toward the sound of my voice,

slumped his shoulders in defeat and lowered his antlers.

"All right. Tell Cervida you found me and I was dead."

"Why would I tell her that?"

"Because I told you to tell her that. I don't want her to see me this way."

"Listen, pal. It's rare when I find a live moose during the killing season and it's even rarer when a moose has a chance to say goodbye before he dies. Cervida's a good cow and this ain't no way to treat a cow."

He nodded his head a few times as he circled and limped and bumped into trees.

"You got a way with words, Gigas."

Then I remembered the other symptom of brainworm and the thought sent a shiver of instinct through my body.

"Wait a minute. Another symptom of brainworm is no fear of humans."

"Yeah," he said, "humans ain't so bad. They don't scare me."

"You run across any lately?"

"Down on the road, just a few minutes ago. A couple of males in a white truck. Seemed like nice fellows."

The gunshot roared from somewhere in the trees. Cervida's male blew out a breath as he stumbled once, and then collapsed. I froze for a moment, stunned by the speed of life to death. I looked into his far away eyes, the blood flowing out his mouth, the familiar scene tearing at me. The second shot pierced my rack, blowing off the tip of one of my tines. My blood spurted in the air and sprayed the trees. I bolted away from the sound of the gun, moving blindly through the forest, ripping down small alders and stomping on the thorny Devil's Club bushes. The forest grew darker as I ran deeper and deeper, my head down, driven by the sick feeling of fear.

I smashed into a big, old spruce tree. My long, skinny legs wobbled back and forth. My head spun into darkness.

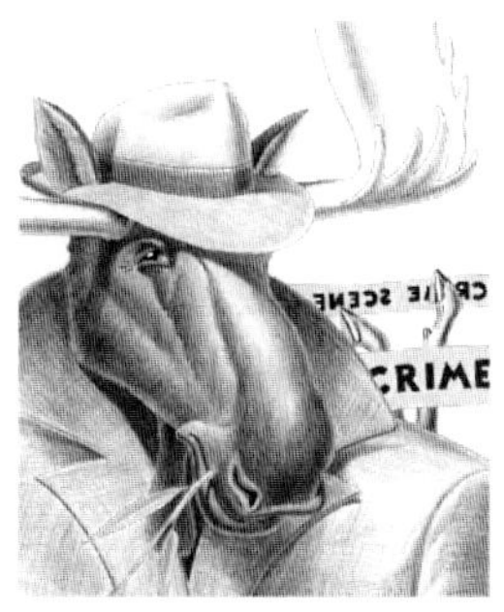

THE NORTH WIND SLAMMED ME, knocking me backwards and off my legs into the river bank. I was blinded by the river silt, blowing into my eyes like hard, horizontal rain. I stood up on my front legs and the wind slapped me back to the ground. I lay there, helpless, pinned to the earth.

The wind stopped. The dust settled as I struggled to stand up. I blinked the dirt out of my eyes and shook my head a few times to clear my vision. The quiet in the valley made my stomachs queasy. I looked up. I was in the middle of the valley and I should have been along the wide, braided Chilkat River but the riverbed was dry. There was no vegetation; not a baby alder tree or a horsetail fern. I looked up higher on the Chilkat Mountains and the forest of spruce and hemlock that once filled the valley was gone. No waterfalls. No snowpack. The Coast Range, once full of glaciers, stood out like dried animal bones.

I hurt from hunger as I wandered down the dusty riverbed. I stumbled over what I thought was a big piece of driftwood. When I was about to kick it out of my way I realized it was a set of decomposing moose antlers. Next to the antlers was the faint outline of tire tracks. As I followed along slowly, examining the tread, I recognized the familiar tire patterns in the dirt. My adrenaline kicked in and I raced along the tracks, running as fast as I could. I ran for miles, my head down, the tracks becoming crystal clear in front of me. I knew I was closing in.

My antlers crashed into the back of the white truck, shattering the glass of the taillights. I dropped to the ground. I smelled the stench of humans and felt them lift me off the ground and into the back of the truck.

"Hi, Al."

I opened my eyes. Sheriff Winkle was standing over me.

"It is what it is, Al, it is what it is."

I woke up, aching in the dark. I heard the stroke of eagle wings over the treetops. The sound of the leaves blowing in the wind tickled my ears.

A flying squirrel was sitting on my antlers.

"WHAT HAPPENED, AL?"

"Looks like a squirrel mugged me."

Rodney was a Southeast Alaskan flying squirrel, a nocturnal resident of the rain forest. He was a special agent of the Squirrel Burrow of Investigation (SBI) and quite a celebrity in the forest world since he cracked the famous Spruce Cone Caper.

Spruce cones are a major part of a squirrel's diet.

One squirrel can store and eat over 16,000 cones a year. When spruce cones began to disappear and there were a series of daring robberies of squirrel caches, the forest roared with the chittering of hungry squirrels. Tempers flared, accusations were made, vigilante justice erupted. Rodney negotiated tense hostage situations as he tried to calm the community. He knew it was an outside job.

Rodney was a master of disguise and he spoke 30 regional squirrel dialects. Posing as a Latvian chipmunk he infiltrated the Russian Rodent Mob. In an action packed, heart stopping, tree top chase through an old growth forest, Stoney battled Boris, the Russian mob leader. Two quick blows from Rodney's lethal tail knocked the rodent gangster from a branch and he plunged two hundred feet to the forest floor, impaling himself on the quills of a local porcupine.

"How did you find me, Rod?"

"Human punk kids have been taking potshots at squirrels so I put together an Automotive Pit Crew Task Force (APCTF) to get under car hoods and chew on wire. We were in the middle of a team meeting a few trees down when I heard the crash."

I wobbled to my feet.

"What do you need from me, Al?"

"I need you to meet me in town later."

"I'm nocturnal, Al. I don't do mornings."

"A moose I was hired to find was killed in the woods a few hours ago. I need to know if anybody saw a truck carrying a stiff moose."

"I've got a couple of crows who are snitches.

If they don't know, they know somebody who does."

Rodney took off flying from tree to tree. I ran ten miles to town. I didn't stop once, even to eat. I came up the hill from the river and looked out over the town. I had walked through the little town many times in the middle of the night. Those had been peaceful times for me; serene moments of what life must have been like before humans walked this land. But it wasn't peaceful to me now. Too much blood had been spilled. I was angry.

And full of revenge.

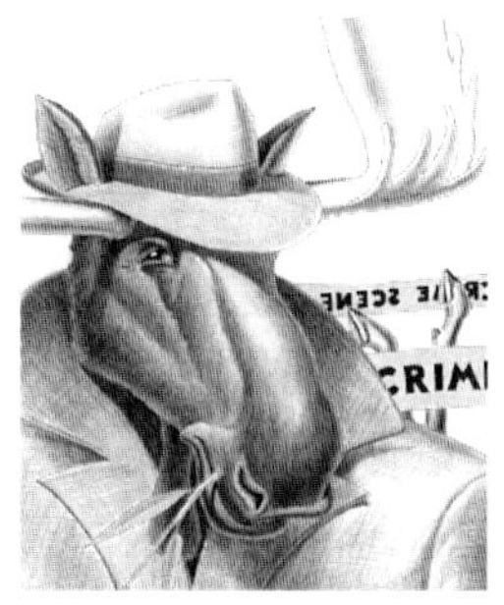

I STOOD UNDER A STREETLIGHT IN front of the bank and looked at my reflection in the windows. The top of my right rack was gone, blown away by the shots in the woods. The crash into the tree had tweaked my rack so the left side of my antlers stuck up higher than the right side. Rain ran down the windows of the bank, giving my reflection a distorted, dreamy appearance, as if my physical wounds symbolized my emotional battle scars.

"Pssst. Caw-caw. Psst. Caw-caw."

I turned around. I could make out the outline of a crow in the shadows. I moved toward him.

"Hold your horses, hoofer," the crow said. "Stoney tells me you're looking for info on a moose kill from last night."

"Who are you?" I asked.

"I'm a black bird of the corvid family, often confused with the raven, known for its raucous sound that doesn't have time for small talk. Go down the street past the grocery store and the school. The first street after the Moose Lodge take a right. Three houses down you'll see a white truck. That's who you're looking for."

"Thanks."

"Don't thank me. As far as anyone is concerned, I wasn't here."

"Who wasn't here?"

"Exactly," the crow said as he flew away.

I walked up Main Street, first light softening the mountains around me. A police car patrolled up and down the street on its nightly route. I stepped back into the shadows by the school and hid behind the totem pole out front. After the car passed I looked both ways, then I ran across the street.

The white truck sat in the driveway. I walked up and looked in the back. The smell of blood and death gagged me and I backed up.

The door of the house opened. A human male stepped outside. With a gun. My survival instinct kicked in and, head down, I charged toward him. My speed surprised him. He tried to back up but he stumbled and fell, the rifle falling out of his reach. He got to his knees and I knocked him over on his back. He stumbled to his feet and ran toward a tree. I could have overtaken him but he was no longer a threat. He jumped for a tree limb, missed and slid down the bark. He tried again with no success. My adrenalin slowed and I was able to think beyond instinct. I stepped toward him and stopped ten feet away. He turned to face me. His eyes opened wide like an owl. I heard a faint sound of water and realized he was urinating.

So, here we were. Fear was now on the other hoof. He was mine—if I wanted him. But, would it bring justice for Cervida's male? Would it stop the killings? Was the sheriff really right, that it is what it is? And what did that really mean? That this human in front of me was destined to kill moose and I was destined to allow it to happen and be a victim of his destiny? That my actions had no effect on the future, that the impact of my time on earth was no more significant than the dust of the decomposing antlers in my dreams?

I looked at the human in front of me, shaking like a baby moose. My anger had filtered out into the wind. Revenge was no longer guiding my consciousness. A feeling of destiny filled me with clarity and peace. I inhaled slowly, then exhaled deeply. "It is what it is," I repeated to myself three times. I bowed my head in honor of all the herbivores in a carnivore world.

Then I charged.